NLP

Why Natural Language Processing Is A Fruitful Scientific Field For Human To Human Communication. Reasons Why You Must Be Familiar With The Hidden NLP Methods For People Understanding And Analysis

(Easy Ways To Boost Your Self-Assurance, Succeed, And Reach Your Full Potential)

Drew Foley

TABLE OF CONTENT

Advantages Of NLP For Those Who Use It.................... 1

Uncertainty About Comprehension............................14

Uncertain Phrasing..28

Consider Visualizing 57

Accept The Expenses And Repercussions Associated With Attaining Your Objective..78

Define Dark Nlp. 105

Utilizing NLP In Mentoring 136

Varieties Of NLP Education..147

In What Way Does Hypnosis Benefit You? 171

Advantages OfNLP For Those Who Use It

A lot of NLP has been eloquently illustrated in the preceding chapters. The various supporters within the system and how it affects various people's lives. Among them are:

• Assists in reducing tension and worry

This kind of natural therapy works well for other people who are experiencing anxiety, and NLP provides similar relief. A study that was done demonstrates how NLP has helped several claustrophobics. The anxiousness was reduced when MRI scans were performed. It lessens tension and anxiety through the application of language mechanisms. When nervous, they can discuss the issue and feel at ease.

- It Enhances Commercial Achievement

NLP has aided in changing behaviours to fit the objectives and goals of businesses and professional careers. It is beneficial without the individual considering how to be a slave to their work and not be productive. The bottom line is that forming new habits helps break bad ones, which leads to commercial success.

- Fosters Creativity

NLP employs methods, tactics, and strategies that foster creativity in its practitioners when you know how several senses affect a person's behaviour. After that, try out various tactics.

- Assists in Vanquishing Phobia and Fear

It concentrates on methods that comprehend tactics and safeguard and improve habits. This aids in altering the internal response and lessens fear and phobias.

- Enhances Relationships and Health

NLP enhances relationships and overall health. It lowers the degree of depression and aids in enhancing coping mechanisms. In actuality, people can transform their vices into virtues. It aids in reducing anxiety, which always has a detrimental impact on one's life and well-being. This idea prioritizes and consistently strives to enhance our comprehension of human behaviour. Interpersonal relationships are enhanced. There is an increased comprehension of the actions and behaviours of others.

Chapter 3: Techniques for NLP

Neural-linguistic programming, or NLP for short, is a psychological communication method. This indicates that the communication method examines the brain and its general functioning. The vocabulary of the communication mode—the neurological component—leads to this conclusion. Every person's brain functions differently and responds to situations in unique ways. Thus, the manner of communication varies across individuals based on their gender, race, age, and even within organizations that they have formed. The entire communication approach emphasizes that each person has unique thoughts and concerns. They could even be identical yet differ in strength. Since each person's brain is uniquely designed or set, it is important to recognize that everyone is unique.

The way communication operates is based on the NLP model. It might work out depending on how the person intending to use it approaches the situation. Psychiatrists are among the specialists who use this form of communication the most. As their profession involves comprehending human emotions and the interplay between the body and mind, this form of communication is appropriate for them to employ. They aim to comprehend how the daily activities of humans impact the functioning of the mind.

So how does the brain function in tandem with the body, one could wonder? First and foremost, the brain responds to commands or actions issued by the body. This also holds for the bodies and minds of animals in various animal kingdoms and classifications. A physical part sends a specific signal to the brain when it needs something, and the brain responds accordingly. This explains how, despite their extreme differences, the body and intellect are programmed to cooperate.

People may read and understand brain activity by scanning their brain waves. These waves explain a person's highs and lows in brain activity. These waves make it easier for someone to understand how humans function. What am I trying to say? For humans to live in harmony and be wonderful beings, their body parts must cooperate. A psychiatrist can read and interpret brain waves. Ultimately, they also share their difficulties with someone and explain how to resolve them.

One must comprehend the brain and communication independently to fully comprehend the communication style linked to the brain. Thus, the art of communication is speaking and listening to others. Communication is two-way: sender to recipient and recipient back to sender. To put it plainly, communication is simple to use and comprehend. Every day, communication takes place everywhere. This phenomenon also affects people, plants, and animals.

For this reason, all animals, plants, and people can communicate with one another. There are other ways to communicate as well, but they are unrelated to the topic at hand right now.

One of the main foundations of a happy, healthy existence is communication.

Every time communication occurs, the brain is involved. What general impact does the brain have on communication, then? That is easy to understand. The brain is represented as a communication triangle before any signals or symbols; it filters and determines the best course of action in every circumstance. This demonstrates how sophisticated and well-organized animal and human communication is. Communication can also be unique and highly engaging depending on what is being discussed and how it is handled by those having the conversation as a whole.

So, how does brain-assisted communication become compelling? This is a difficult issue to answer, but obviously, the physical components assist the brain in shaping communication into whatever it sees fit. The ears, eyes, and tongue, in particular, are examples of these physical components. To keep the conversation interesting, it's important to know and comprehend the recipient's interests so that you can keep the conversation moving in that direction. One needs to ask themselves some questions for this to occur. Among these are the following: how can the recipient give the conversation their whole attention? How can I maintain the recipient's interest without making them feel bored? These are a few strategies for maintaining good relations between the sender and the recipient in any communication process.

Lastly, how can we apply and comprehend NLP in our day-to-day activities? This is an excellent question to comprehend the brain's and communication's value. This type of communication relies heavily on the brain. Since the brain, or a certain lobe within it, is the centre of all communication, all answers are formed and understood there. Nonverbal language processing (NLP) facilitates comprehension of communication by removing uncertainty about the process and mode of communication. Only those who have received specialized training and education in studying human, animal, or possibly both brains are qualified to use this form of communication. The NLP is for the select few to utilize, not for everyone. Because it is mostly performed on subjects who consent, it is also restricted to a very small number of people.

Understanding NLP requires knowledge of its techniques as well as an understanding of how it operates. The communication method needs to function in a certain way. Its methods clarify how it operates, its benefits and drawbacks. These enable us to determine its application and non-application areas. Psychiatrists have provided several strategies for navigating NLP; we will approach it broadly and impartially. This is to help the reader grasp and get a clear picture of NLP.

Uncertainty About Comprehension

This won't help if, for example, you are perplexed by quantum physics and know nothing about it, have read very little about it, and have only heard vague references to it. All it will do is show you there is no data for the "understand" program to process.

On the other hand, the "understand" programme will assist you in making sense of the data or information if you have obtained it and are putting it through a programme with a negative motif (like the confusion programme).

We'll begin with a practice to help you see and hear differences in the internal conversation and pictures. Then, we'll implement these adjustments more smoothly and effortlessly. Even though we exclude taste, smell, and touch, this method works well.

You will also have the resources to help you get unstuck if you ever get stuck because you will understand the basic blocks after doing this.

Work out

Consider an issue that you are unclear about. Regarding the visual, auditory, and internal noise, take note of:

Visual

1. Where are you in space?

2. How big is the main object and the image size?

3. How far away is the image from you?

4. Connected, separated, or unconnected?

5. Is the picture surrounded by a frame?

6. Vibrance?

7. Is it in colour or just monochrome?

8. Pay attention.

9. Is it stationary or in motion?

10. A single image or several?

11. Does attention fluctuate?

12. Is it three-dimensional?

13. Slant?

14. Consistency? (Losing a picture, splitting up, etc.)

15. How does the image look?

1. Location with relation to space. Where is the picture when you look at your visual representation when you consider the topic confusing? Make a point of it. That's not just nodding your head in the general direction; it's lifting your hand and pointing. Most people draw their images in three dimensions: up, down, left, right, or directly in front of them. People occasionally see the image as they imagine it. POINT ANYWAY.

Examine each item on the list and take notes.

2. Dimensions. "Is it life-size, larger, or smaller than life?" is my first question. Get the size, either 3 feet by 2 feet, half-life size, or whatever you can determine if it's bigger or smaller than life. I'm presuming that you're improving yourself.

3. Distinction. Given that the image is in space, what is its distance from you?

4. Connected or disconnected. You are linked if the visual representation makes you feel as though you are in the image

and experiencing it. You are detached if you feel as though you are gazing at yourself "out there" while staring at an image that appears to have been captured by a camera. You are detached if you are not staring at a picture of yourself, AND you are not in the picture (if you can only see your hands and not your face or the back of your head). The pictures usually have the highest emotional intensity while you are associated, the lowest when you are dissociated, and the lowest when you are detached.

Copying Your Nonverbal Cues

Therefore, the first concept we will examine is that of the manipulator or the person who uses NLP techniques to aid themselves by copying body language. Individuals skilled in utilising these strategies will begin to imitate the victim's body language. This gives the victim the impression that they are closer to the manipulator, even though they frequently aren't aware that this is the case.

Therefore, the NLP user will act in the same way as the victim if they are standing with their hand on their hip. The NLP user will act similarly if the victim exudes excessive confidence, crosses their arms slightly, and puffs out their chest. The key takeaway is that the manipulator will closely observe their victim and their body language, then replicate it. This facilitates the development of a relationship between the manipulator and the victim by demonstrating to the victim that they can rely on and trust the manipulator.

A skilled NLP manipulator may be able to begin speaking with the victim in this way in certain situations. Therefore, if someone is extremely enthusiastic, the NLP user may feed off that enthusiasm, projecting a positive attitude and general happiness. From a personality perspective, this can also go the other way. The manipulator will attempt to mimic this and radiate the same mindset if they encounter someone who appears more pessimistic, frequently complains, and enjoys sharing bad opinions.

The manipulator could even take advantage of the other person's sense of touch to establish a greater connection. Although this may seem a little offensive, some people find this kind of touch so off-putting that they fail to recognise the manipulation that is taking place. This frequently occurs in both professional and educational settings. A supervisor or teacher may approach from behind the employee or pupil and put their hand on their shoulder. Although this may appear amicable at first, it is frequently a tactic used to control the victim or the other person. Most people, including victims, will consent to the other person touching them to prevent discomfort. Only by employing contact could the manipulator increase their authority while the victim was trying to avoid a scene.

Try doing some odd things you wouldn't normally do, and then watch if the other person is working on the same thing to ensure that they aren't copying your movements or attempting to use NLP on you. Perhaps you could discover a humorous hand trick to perform, such as lightly tapping the top of your head while you speak. You can tilt your head back and forth or quickly shift your gaze around.

There's a good chance the other person is attempting to manipulate you with some NLP techniques if you notice that they are doing things unusual for you.

You can use the same strategy with anyone who tries to touch you at work or during a chat. Don't just stay silent if you don't want to be affected by this person; take a moment to confront them immediately. If you ask them nicely to stop, they will typically quit and not do it again, so you don't have to make a big deal.

It is imperative to acknowledge that certain individuals tend to emulate the mannerisms and behaviours of persons in their immediate vicinity due to ingrained personality traits. This is less of a manipulative strategy and more of a codependency. You might need to take a closer look at the other person and determine what they stand to gain from the circumstance to determine their genuine motivations. It is a clue that their behaviour is harmless if they don't appear to be stealing anything from you while they do it.

Chilled Interpretation

An additional outcome of using NLP techniques is a procedure called "cold reading." At this point, the manipulator will attempt to persuade you that they already know more than you do. Already, many engage in this practice, such as mediums, psychics, fortune tellers, and mentalists. They will use it to give the impression that the victim is more aware of particular details than they are. People with exceptional reading comprehension skills may rapidly discern your nonverbal signs and body language, enabling them to comprehend your methods and essence. From there, they can make several educated guesses to infer details, examine your body language and other responses from the victim, and determine whether or not they are correct.

A psychic might, for instance, begin by telling a gathering of people that they are conversing with someone whose name starts with the letter J. Given that most of the audience probably knew someone who passed away and had the last name J, these people may have assumed the psychic was speaking about someone they knew. A spectator might even break the conversation and share something like, "My uncle Jason just passed away." After that, the magician will follow that audience member, interpreting their nonverbal cues to make a few sweeping generalisations that the audience member can apply to their own lives.

Uncertain Phrasing

Gibberish will appeal to those who enjoy using NLP techniques. To slip in the true meaning of what they want to say to the victim, they will either say a few short phrases or conceal particular words in long sentences. This is something that commercials frequently depict. There can be too much information available. Pay attention to a commercial that promotes one drug over another. In this one, the entire conversation will centre around the medication and how wonderful it is. Then, in the final moments, usually only a few, there will be a quick reading that includes all of the advice and cautions a patient needs to be aware of before taking that medication.

We also witness this behaviour in the many ways we engage with individuals. You'll discover that younger children—even teenagers—can be helpful in this regard. They might start by listing why someone might grant their request before requesting permission to obtain or perform something. Afterwards, they will expeditiously review any grounds for rejection provided by the parent or another individual.

When using NLP, a person will make sure to speak very ambiguously. They might employ rapid-fire jargon to divert your attention or use language so vague that you can't follow through on any of the ideas or concepts, leaving you perplexed about their true intentions. Several of the political expressions that have gained popularity over time serve as a great illustration of this. Obama ran on the "Change" platform, which is appealing to everyone. Numerous manipulators can also make use of this. They will continue to use ambiguous phrases to please most people in their immediate vicinity.

These manipulators may make statements like "I'll take care of it," but they never provide suggestions or an explanation for how they plan to resolve the issue. Then, additional manipulators can keep providing general facts and omit any details that could change the victim's opinion.

Chapter 3: Understanding NLP and Using It Effectively

Relationship building and communication are the two most important things in life. You can establish rapport with anyone in both your personal and professional life with the use of NLP. You can establish a connection with someone by observing their communication style, body language, and breathing patterns. You may simply mimic the other person's behaviour after you learn to pay attention to them, which will facilitate the development of a rapport.

Among the most significant NLP approaches is this one. Even though this method was previously included in the list, I believe it merits repeating because it was important in the early stages of neuro-linguistic programming.

If the practitioner doesn't build rapport with the client beforehand, they can't use NLP on them. How are you going to accomplish this? Check out the list that follows.

Make the customer feel at ease.

Let them talk about him.

Never cut someone else off while they are speaking.

Never pass judgment.

Give advice only upon request.

Making the other person like you right away is the main goal. You won't be able to connect with him or her and affect them if you can't accomplish this.

This is where developing a rapport's foundation (27) is important. As a practitioner, you are responsible for matching your client's physiology, tone, words, and actions. Once you can accomplish this, a solid rapport built on mutual respect and trust will be built, which will eventually help to facilitate NLP.

You may build a rapport with your clientele quickly if you adhere to these pointers. You must remember this when building a relationship with your client.

You cannot execute NLP at all if you cannot do this.

Pacing is a technique that uses the idea that people prefer similarities. Thus, we can quickly build rapport by resembling ourselves to others. Mirroring and matching are the first steps in the pacing process.

We mimic their gestures and body language by matching. We raise our left hands in response to his raising his left. We mimic whatever the other person does when we mirror them, but we do it more like a reflection in a mirror. We raise our right hand if he raises his left. Mirroring and matching are imitations of other people's actions.

If we did something simple, we could instantly establish rapport with someone else. However, a lot of people had trouble establishing rapport with this method. Why? Mainly because they only operate at the physiology stage. We need to match other things besides mirroring and matching their physique.

Start by matching their voice characteristics, such as pitch, pace, loudness, and tone. In case they speak loudly, you should likewise speak loudly. You must speak at the same tempo as them if they speak quickly. And so forth.

It's also crucial to match their pace of respiration. Observing their breathing patterns, tempo, and location (chest, diaphragm, or abdomen) is important.

This is a little challenging. You can get practice by viewing a silent film.

Then, matching their sensory predicate is crucial. Predicates serve as a person's primary or preferred representational system when speaking. Thus, we will encounter individuals who are visual, auditory, kinesthetic, and auditory digital types.

Some people find comprehending, remembering, and making judgments using their visual senses easier. They will, therefore, employ a predicate that is probably dominated by the visual sense, such as:

1. It's quite evident to me what you mean.

2. The future appears promising.

We will also encounter kinesthetic and auditory individuals. Predicates that access the aural sense are used by auditory people, such as:

1. I've never heard of it before.

2. I think your suggestion is a good one.

As for kinesthetic individuals:

1. Something doesn't feel right.

2. The film was quite moving.

Apart from the trio above, an additional category is auditory digital. The digital auditory is not the same as the analogue one. While auditory digital involves the meaning of words and symbols, the auditory representation system deals with actual sound. Auditory digital people use words and phrases that don't refer to any representational system:

1. I get what you're saying.

2. For now, I'm still calculating the cost-benefit.

Note, however, that this does not imply that one individual uses a single representation! Therefore, it doesn't follow that visual types don't use kinesthetic or auditory predicates. They simply prefer visual predicates over others, while they also utilize kinesthetic or auditory ones.

It is hard to determine someone's preferred representational system while speaking, is it? Instead, we need to employ a questionnaire. Thus, the following indicators can be used to determine someone's preferred system!

visual style

1. Talk loudly and quickly. Speak without pausing occasionally.

2. It has a tidy and appealing appearance.

3. They usually take in air through their upper lungs.

4. Their eyes look to the top left or right when thinking.

5. Predicates that access visual senses are employed. See, glance, watch, appear, view, envision, observations, lovely, bright, and so forth are a few examples.

type of auditory

1. Talk at a moderate pace. Occasionally lyrical and fond of whispering.

2. It has a straightforward, uncomplicated appearance.

3. Take a breath in the centre of your chest.

4. Their eyes shift to the left or right when they ponder.

5. The utilization of auditory senses is the predicate. For instance, ringing, loud, ask, speak, give an ear, and so forth.

Kinesthetic category

1. Talk slowly and in a low tone.

2. Don't worry about their appearance if it makes them feel comfortable.

3. inhale deeply from their chests.

4. Their gaze shifts to the bottom right as they consider.

5. Kinesthetic senses are accessed as the predicate. A few examples are touch, feel, safe, serene, comfort, connect, make contact, and so forth.

Digital audio format

A little trickier to recognize is the auditory digital type:

1. There are moments when the speech rate is sluggish.

2. From your lower abdomen, breathe.

3. Their gaze is to the bottom left when they are thinking.

4. The employed predicates are abstract and have no direct sensory connection. As an illustration, examine the following: choose, experience, learn, process, think, comprehend, evaluate, perceive, insensitive, conceive, compute, and so forth.

5. Frequently less emotionally invested in the results.

You can use those indicators to ascertain someone's favourite method. You can interact effectively with him if you can determine their favourite system, which begs the next question: "Why do I need to know their preferred system?" Their preferred system just requires you to utilize the same predicates, so you may stop having them decode your words.

A visual person is likely not to hear you if you approach them with a suggestion or say, "Hey, listen to my opinion." This is because they are visual learners. Therefore, it would be far better if you said, "I've seen things from your perspective and I have an idea." I'm sure this would grab their attention.

Using the same predicates will make it easier for you to establish rapport with them and for them to comprehend your objectives.

Therefore, we can mimic and replicate their speech qualities, breathing patterns, body posture and gesture, and sensory predicates to swiftly establish rapport. We unintentionally communicate with the other person when we act in this way. In reality, you're saying, "Hey, you and I are the same. You should feel safe, calm, and comfortable."

Naturally, without me saying so, you must not imitate or mimic their embarrassing actions, such as accents, stuttering, limping, etc.

You can begin persuading them once you've built rapport with them. You can begin promoting your goods if you work in sales. As a manager, you can start delegating responsibilities to your staff members. You can start asking someone out if you have a crush on her.

However, how can I tell whether we've developed a rapport? How can I tell if I and the other person are getting along well?

Eventually, abruptly alter your position and observe their reaction. Once you've built rapport, they will unintentionally adopt the same or similar position. You could try it three times, at least to be certain.

Additionally, if you hear them say something like, "It's so nice talking with you," or "I feel like I've known you for a long time," It's clear that a rapport has been built.

Finally, I would advise you to always establish rapport with the best intentions! Not only do we communicate verbally and through language when we communicate, but we also communicate subconsciously. Even if someone tries to hide it, the other person can see whether someone is conversing with malice.

Many people, particularly in the activist communities for women, have denounced the use of NLP as a luring tool. They say it takes away people's decision-making ability and makes them do things they wouldn't normally agree to. The argument made in opposition to this viewpoint is that NLP can be used to significantly enhance a meaningful experience and help people feel a wider range of positive feelings. Most people who use NLP for meaningful purposes do so with true intentions. Not the thoughts themselves, but the few who don't are to blame for despicable intentions.

The long-term model of demonstrating NLP has also been criticized. It has been said that the environment in which NLP is taught is similar to a clique since people are encouraged to accept the NLP standards without question and refrain from participating in important decisions. Opponents assure that NLP accreditations are granted without adequate testing or careful planning. NLP, demonstrating that schools have been hit,

resisted this approach and, after some consideration, insisted that people be free to accept or reject the information they are taught and that NLP instructors have no means of restricting free thought. They also insist that people only obtain an NLO certificate when they are ready, and the conventional therapy sector has responded to this by highlighting the negative aspects of NLP.

Recognize Your Principles

Now that you have established your desired outcome, you have deeply related it to the daily motivations that propel you forward. This is great, but to greatly increase your chances of developing self-discipline, you should list your strengths and compare them to the results you hope to achieve.

Since this is a personal matter, there's no point in advising you on certain values to consider. Just think about the things in life that impact you most. Some people note that it helps to pretend you are a candidate for a political position. Which issues are the focus of your mission? What assurances do you give the people? This is a powerful exercise to help you identify your main principles.

After listing all of your important attributes, you should prioritize them in descending order of strength, just as you ranked your drives previously. You should list each of your top three attributes separately after you have outlined them.

It's time to connect your attributes to your drives and outcomes. You may be sure that you are focused on achieving your goal at a deep, subconscious level by ensuring all three components are in place. Take into consideration a big motivator for you, like sincerity. At that point, you may envision how it fits your goal and drive. For example, you can believe your delight target will be satisfied if you are consistently legitimate. This helps to ensure that all of your inspirations are enhancing one another rather than living independently.

Motivation changes, but habits don't

motivate, as previously expressed. In the unlikely event that you have not taken action

Go back to the section above and complete it right away. You must finish the two tasks before moving on. After that, you're ready to outline the two key pillars of support that the rest of your discipline is built upon, providing inspiration and inclinations. Both are essential to advancing you toward your goals. The key difference between the two is that propensities are more carefully laid out yet have a longer lifespan. In contrast, inspiration is quicker but has a more constrained lifespan.

You should consider all the ways that achieving your goal will make you feel amazing to convince yourself of its success. Consider the scenario when you are trying to get promoted at work. Think about the practical changes that will come about in your life when you complete the advancement, but also consider how these advancements relate to deeper viewpoints such as emotions and values. For the time being, we shall examine this cycle using an example.

For example, let's imagine that after completing your

progress, you've received a wage increase. Take a moment to visualize this event and allow it to seem real. How does it make you feel to imagine it?

Perhaps the extra money has given you stronger security and genuine peace. Perhaps you feel opportunity more strongly now that you know you won't veer into the red in the future. Whatever it may be, be sure to locate it. Anything you feel matters; all you need to do is ensure you have a valid understanding of the feelings that achieving your goal will arouse.

You can be convinced to pursue your goal if you have a realistic idea of what it will mean for you and the difference it will make in your life. This will give you a more positive attitude on starting it.

As previously said, inspiration is not difficult to achieve but is not sustained over an extended period. Therefore, it's crucial to create habits that support your outcome. If you don't make a conscious effort to change your tendencies, you'll end up with designs that don't support your outcomes and values in day-to-day living. To create beneficial habits, you should first think about the actions you should do overall to

reach your goal. For instance, you might need to start tracking your spending and creating a budget if your objective is to save more money. Then, these behaviours can be broken down into a more manageable set of specific routines.

To create a financial plan, for example, you may need to track your investments over time, including the total, and divide the amount into other categories. You may need to retrain your mind to look for ways to cut costs, such as when shopping and coming across amazing deals. The tendency to modify your budget about your income may need to be framed as part of a larger spending strategy.

It goes beyond simply listing tendencies and sources of inspiration for detachment. It's necessary to connect them. You may achieve this by ensuring your inspiration aligns with the habits you want to maintain regularly. The NLP security approach can support this. For example, you could activate your inspiration by visualizing the good feelings that will arise from reaching your goal. Next, as you do your daily activity, you would make a repetitive bodily motion, like caressing your left wrist. This connects the inspiration feeling subliminally to the movement itself. Once the wrist touch trigger is down, you may initiate the inspiration feeling on command.

Consider Visualizing

By picturing something, one can better comprehend how to bring it to life. Additionally, it acquaints the mind with the concept, forming the mental habit of perceiving the imagined as actuality. Your mind develops an eagerness to acknowledge this fact.

NLP routinely employs visualization. Certain categories of NLP visualization are, in fact, quite abstract, as will become apparent in the course of discussing subsequent techniques within this section. Others, however, are quite straightforward. Merely imagining the realization of one's objectives and experiencing success in life is sufficient to manifest those objectives. By visualizing what you wish to accomplish or acquire, you prepare yourself to manifest a desire. You will become so enthralled by what you see that you will try to attain it. Your mind will acknowledge it as a plausible reality, facilitating attaining your desired outcomes.

Visualization requires an intense desire to create every detail. You intend to concentrate on a particular subject until it becomes an all-encompassing image that resembles reality. The greater the amount of time devoted to visualization, the more tangible and precise one's vision may appear.

Reduce the Size of Things in Your Mind

Humans have a mental propensity to exaggerate situations. Particularly distressing or painful occurrences and concerns may appear enormous in one's mind. They can even overshadow everything else if you devote excessive effort and concentration to them.

Engaging in the process of mental reduction can significantly facilitate overcoming specific concerns or occurrences. Visualize the significant entity, occurrence, or individual as an image within a frame. On a computer screen, particular events or sequences can be visualized as movie segments within dialogue boxes. The image may be rendered in black and white if doing so facilitates its disassociation.

Presently, envision the image or dialogue box diminishing in size until it vanishes entirely.

Engaging in such imagery instructs the mind to reduce the size of objects it erupts. It might be necessary to repeatedly visualize this imagery for it to be effective. If the process takes an extended period, avoid becoming disheartened or giving up. This is mental training, and it may require some time to penetrate your mind. Employ moving picture imagery to diminish the magnitude of your negative thoughts and concerns whenever you begin catastrophizing.

Perform Actions Backwards

Reenacting events in reverse can be an effective strategy for those who are having difficulty recovering from a traumatic experience. Visualize the instant when the distressing incident came to an end. Proceed to replay the remaining events in a sequential fashion but in reverse. By doing so, the trauma associated with the event can be extracted, allowing the mind to gradually embrace it as an ordinary occurrence rather than a traumatic one. Engaging in backward playback can facilitate cognitive processing.

Consider Vivid Colors

Visualizing a particular emotion, such as pleasure or confidence, can be beneficial as a colour if you wish to experience that emotion more frequently. For instance, red, yellow, or any other hue that one associates with pleasure could represent happiness. Colours that evoke a personal response should always be chosen, unlike those that society associates with particular emotions. Including your associations in this exercise will significantly increase its effectiveness.

Imagine yourself now standing in front of a massive square of colour. Consider entering the plaza. The moment your feet enter the square, the emotion begins to permeate your soles and each cell of your body. Currently, the emotion associated with the colour permeates and transforms you.

It is possible to envision this to experience a specific emotion. It is an excellent method to boost your confidence or cheer yourself up before a frightening event, such as a speech.

Methods by Which NLP Is Evident

One instance is that deceit may constitute an attribute of improper human conduct. Nevertheless, identical fabrications can be employed in an alternative manner that may not be morally abhorrent. Consider two actors who collaborate on a film. They will behave like a father and son, spouse and wife, or romantic couple. This behaviour affects the NLP in a manner analogous to if the situation were factually accurate, albeit with a shift in context; in fact, it can be considered a form of deception. It is imperative to employ appropriate context when relevant; however, it is critical to avoid tarnishing the humanity of others, as the human mind is a priceless asset, and individuals ought not to compromise their human values under any circumstances.

A further technique is chunking. Chunking, which translates to "cutting something into small pieces," refers in NLP to how individuals design structured, formal, and approachable learning environments to retain the material in daily life. It is acceptable to attempt to complete a 200-page book; however, it may be impractical for two to three days, and doing so may be detrimental to your health. What NLP teaches us is more akin to deconstructing a book into chapters and finishing it within ten to fifteen days. Read a section of the book each day until it is finished. Likewise, on the first day, bodybuilders who wish to alter their physique cannot construct it through callisthenics and hundreds of push-ups and pull-ups. Daily, they methodically construct their musculature. They engage in coordinated muscle development by beginning with abdominal exercises and progressing to arms and leg exercises. They eventually attain the physique of a bodybuilder through this process. Contributions from NLP instructors and other individuals rendered the program organized and approachable. They divided lengthy tasks into more manageable segments, enabling students to comprehend and derive advantages from the concepts introduced in more manageable sections.

Another method of assessing an individual's NLP is by examining their shortcomings. While some consider failure a stepping stone to success, others consider it nothing more than a stone. A "false evidence that appears real" is the source of concern. Cynicism and fear of failure are neither warranted. Refraining from harbouring pessimistic thoughts and viewing setbacks as valuable learning opportunities is advisable. We endeavour to gain knowledge from the feedback we receive, and by doing so, we can impart that knowledge to our successors. An additional approach to managing failure entails perpetually perceiving the positive aspects of the failure itself. While some may perceive a glass as vacant, we should perpetually consider it full. Presently, some clinicians advise against employing cynical justifications such as "I cannot, therefore I will not." Instead, we should devise a strategy to attain the desired outcome. Even if we fail to achieve that objective, we can still gain knowledge by focusing on it.

Ultimately, NLP suggests that we should develop the mental capacity to perceive things differently than intended. Consider how you and another individual perceive a comparable image, and then reevaluate the image from a different vantage point. We should cultivate the cognitive ability to perceive things from perspectives other than our own.

All of these are fundamental perspectives on NLP. In conclusion, I addressed the NLP "essential," also called the NLP presupposition, and chunking, which involves dividing the more significant portions into smaller portions. I proposed that we should consistently strive to find the good in every circumstance, that failure does not exist, and that honing our cognitive ability to perceive possibilities beyond our current limitations is crucial. Each of these behaviours, irrespective of context and substance, is beneficial. I concluded that individuals possess internal resources, with only a catalyst absent. This catalyst becomes apparent to individuals who receive NLP training or consume content related to NLP.

We appreciate your attention. Attaining comprehensive comprehension and application of this program is imperative; therefore, I am convinced that its completion will yield numerous advantages. Proceed to the remaining sessions and collaborate with me on them. Disclosure is encouraged; an email address has been included in the preface. I strongly encourage anyone with inquiries to approach me. I am confident that you will find the series beneficial; in addition to discussing theory, I will illustrate it with examples from my own life. For instance, speaking in front of a group and conversing with women were my greatest fears, but I surmounted them both with the assistance of NLP and diagnostic therapy. Consequently, I desire that individuals gain knowledge from this chapter to impart the insights to their successors.

Additional well-known indicators of dread include hands that are icy and damp, perspiration, laboured or heavy breathing, clenching of the jaw or fist, and possibly closed eyes. The act of an individual lowering their head signifies submission. Even the most formidable aggressor will submit and bow their shoulders when they feel frightened and subjugated by a powerful individual.

The final principle that will be examined in this chapter concerns respiration.

Monitoring respiration is among the most challenging indicators to look for. Different mental and emotional states can be correlated with identical respiration patterns.

A person currently at ease and calm will breathe consistently, albeit with a relatively shallow inhalation and exhalation. A person generally at ease in their surroundings will occasionally exhale deeply or even breathe to increase the amount of oxygen in their system.

However, circumstances alter when an individual experiences a shift in emotion.

Let's start with an individual who is experiencing anxiety. Irritation and anxiety are characterized by inadequate respiration. Panting may be apparent, but this is typically the result of extreme anxiety. Conversely, an elevated rate of inadequate respiration shall be an unmistakable sign that an anomaly has arisen.

Additionally, respiration depression is an indication of distress. This phenomenon is commonly linked to the frozen response. Consequently, a state in which an individual forgets to breathe can be attributed to extreme distress, which causes the body to interrupt specific functions to express discomfort.

Additionally, give close attention to the chest or back of your interlocutor. If their thorax appears to be barely twitching, they are likely breathing shallowly. Observing them breathe through their mouth could indicate that they are engaged in mischievous activity.

There is a tendency for liars to maintain their respiration. This is indicated by the fact that they frequently exhale deeply or breathe frequently. Consequently, even the act of inhaling itself may indicate that something is amiss.

Regardless of how skilled they are at lying, a person who is lying will almost always have extremely shallow respiration. Therefore, consistent deep respiration is a reliable indicator that an individual is being truthful. When people tell the truth, their respiration will remain constant, even if altered.

The principles deliberated upon in this chapter can assist you in attaining a more profound comprehension of largely imperceptible indications and cues that individuals in your vicinity may divulge under specific conditions. Consequently, it is further critical that you remain vigilant whenever you experience feelings of nervousness, anxiety, or even fear. While there is nothing inherently wrong with experiencing particular emotions, exercising caution in concealing one's sentiments will undoubtedly prove beneficial.

Akin to the strategy employed by seasoned poker players, maintaining emotional composure can confer a competitive advantage in sales meetings, job interviews, and negotiations. Ultimately, your capacity to regulate your emotions will contribute to your proficiency as a communicator. Furthermore, your capacity to empathize with others will empower you to attain the status of an accomplished communicator.

Subsequent chapters will examine extremely particular contextual cues that will assist you in discerning the concealed significance that underpins the words and deeds of others. Indeed, you will have the opportunity to acquire a more profound understanding of your conversation partners' emotions or what they sincerely desire to convey but may be incapable of expressing emotionally.

Therefore, I kindly request that you be mindful of your interactions with individuals in your vicinity. Kindly observe their respiration, bodily movements, and facial expressions (or lack thereof). One may record their observations in a journal or their mind. Observing the conduct of others in specific circumstances will enable you to develop an astute understanding of the principles expounded in this chapter. Most significantly, you will develop the ability to formulate your hypotheses regarding the behaviour of others in particular situations.

Hence, try to acquaint yourself with the quirks and gestures of the individuals you interact with. Additionally, be more aware of your movements and demeanour. You may discover that you are revealing considerably more than you initially perceive. Therefore, it is highly advantageous to closely monitor one's movements and behaviours.

Accept The Expenses And Repercussions Associated With Attaining Your Objective.

How will realizing your objective influence various facets of your life and those around you? Furthermore, what are the societal and environmental implications?

Will the results be worthwhile because of the time, effort, and resources invested?

What are the potential benefits of falling short of attaining the intended result?

Is it feasible to integrate the favourable aspects of your current circumstances into your objective?

Contemplate oneself successfully attaining the desired outcome. What observations are made from this external vantage point? Make every effort to experience it as if it were occurring now. Do any distinctions exist? Determine who will be impacted by accomplishing your objective, and then envision your triumph from their perspective. Are you receiving any new information at this time? Gandhi employed this tactic in preparation for negotiations, enabling him to empathize with all parties' concerns.

Should it be feasible to accomplish your objectives at this moment, would you do so? If the answer is no, adjust until the desired result is achieved.

Do you possess every resource necessary to accomplish your objective?

Which resources do you possess that can assist you in attaining your objective? Information, abilities and training, internal emotional state, attitude, funds, external support, and so forth are examples of resources.

Which resources are necessary? How are they to be generated?

In what ways could you modify the situation to reach your objective? Define precisely.

Do you possess a sufficient desire to attain your desired outcome to succeed? In that case, what would inspire you to pursue your objectives?

Are you certain that the initial measure toward accomplishing your objective is precise and feasible?

Have you initiated any actions in pursuit of accomplishing your objective?

Imagine yourself in the future, having accomplished your intended objective. Reflect upon the sequence of events that transpired to recall the surpassed milestones.

Utilizing NLP in Daily Life

NLP has found extensive application in the domains of stress management, communication skill enhancement, empathy cultivation, destructive relationship pattern resolution, and motivational support for individuals experiencing feelings of hopelessness, worthlessness, and helplessness. With this in mind, the technique can accomplish virtually any objective one desires. It can be utilized to break bad habits, exert influence over others, achieve success, lose weight, win back an ex, seduce, earn money, and in virtually any other circumstance that one may encounter in life. A few instances in which NLP can be utilized daily will be discussed.

To begin with, NLP fosters an individual's process of self-exploration. Therefore, applying the instructed processes enables you to develop your comprehension to attain awareness.

This will significantly assist you in comprehending both yourself and others in any circumstance, allowing you to seek professional and personal assistance.

The two primary domains of NLP are self-improvement and empowerment through communication and exerting influence over others. One can exert influence over the decisions of others by employing non-verbal communication strategies and language techniques that have been meticulously crafted. Thus, managers, salespeople, and negotiators can utilize NLP to enhance their business expertise.

In numerous organizations, the perpetual predicament lies in attracting high achievers amidst many average employees. NLP can assist in emulating these high achievers by modifying their thoughts, actions, and routines to facilitate success. The process by which these behaviours and routines are established is called "programming."

Utilizing NLP language patterns in your current environment can enhance communication, leading to greater influence and comprehension. Certain techniques, including mirroring and matching, can be employed to foster and develop a stronger rapport, particularly in situations where immediate rapport is of the utmost importance.

Suppose you experience anxieties, low self-esteem, or other emotional difficulties. You may benefit from implementing certain NLP techniques, such as modifying swish patterns or sub-modalities, as they are highly productive.

In addition to writing, NLP is highly beneficial in the following domains: business, management, consulting, health professions, parenting, athletics, creative endeavours, and sales. In essence, effective communication and achievement hold equivalent significance. In the business world, straightforward NLP abilities that promote progress in rapport-building, goal-setting, and communication are all applicable. Furthermore, it has been demonstrated that NLP is highly effective at assisting individuals in achieving rapid and enduring transformations.

Conversely, NLP can also be utilized by artists, performers, and writers to gain invaluable insight into the creative process. Considering this, one can utilize NLP techniques to inspire and liberate creativity. NLP has numerous practical applications, including developing strategies for educators and learners and comprehending acquired knowledge. Using NLP, teachers and parents can acquire effective strategies to assist their children's academic success. Educators may also incorporate NLP into their pedagogical approaches and utilize it to administer lessons.

An additional advantage of NLP is that it can be applied to personal transformation. NLP facilitates the diversion of attention from limiting beliefs, old habits, and specific anxieties, enabling the development of novel and inspiring strategies for confronting life's challenges. This is because NLP provides more options regarding your responses, emotions, and communication, enabling you to make more informed choices.

Lastly, NLP can also be applied to health. Personal use of NLP is not limited to maintaining health. NLP is also an excellent resource for medical professionals seeking to improve communication with patients and coworkers. Additionally, NLP is applied to developing and maintaining positive thoughts and personal health, utilizing the body's healing capabilities, and explaining the relationship between beliefs and health.

Sixth Principle: Liking

You will, without a doubt, concur with my statement that you prefer to work with individuals you like rather than those you despise.

When I visit a store where I frequently make purchases, I prefer to be assisted by the same sales associates who have previously impressed me. Numerous times, when other salespeople attended to me, but I did not make a purchase, I purchased the same product during my subsequent visit because the salesperson demonstrated it to me, and I found it appealing. Undoubtedly, you have encountered this circumstance at some juncture in your lifetime.

Therefore, to convince someone, it is critical that they like you. One can employ various NLP techniques (e.g., the matching and mirroring technique) to establish rapport with another individual and gain sympathy. Further elaboration on this subject can be obtained by consulting my additional books. At this time, maintaining a pleasant demeanour and a cheerful countenance are the most straightforward methods of establishing a positive rapport with others. Develop your personality and communication abilities to the extent that an individual would be interested in hearing you out and providing a response.

This principle is so fundamental to persuasion that it would be impossible to convince the other person to be persuaded, even if you were the authoritative figure and they disliked you. This demonstrates the critical nature of this principle.

Focus on developing strategies to pique the interest of others. Behave by your audience's analysis; satisfy their requirements by treating them as your own. Be observant and search for cues that will assist you in initiating a conversation with them; a positive exchange of ideas inevitably results in the other person developing a favourable opinion of you.

Everything in this world is extremely significant in persuasion and can have a profound effect. Regrettably, many individuals have disregarded their efforts, which has prevented them from ever determining the cause of their inability to convince and persuade consumers.

As you near the conclusion of the previous principle, you are aware of your current obligation. As the chapters progress, I shall expound upon the methods to enhance the efficacy of your persuasion and refine your application of these principles.

Implementing NLP to Enhance Your Self-Concept

Once you have responded to each of the inquiries above, it is now appropriate to integrate everything. Can you discern the positive and negative characteristics that comprise your self-concept? Despite self-perceived success, can any aspects of one's self-concept be enhanced?

A straightforward illustration of how NLP can assist you in enhancing your self-concept follows. You may have realized that your negative demeanour contributes to your misery. Applying neuro-linguistic programming may reduce one's propensity for temper tantrums and increase patience.

If you have identified the source of your anger, you might conclude that it is excessive. Accepting the possibility that you have a foul temper can facilitate the use of NLP to find a resolution. This is because you have previously recognized the issue within your self-concept.

There are numerous NLP-based methods for enhancing one's self-concept. One may use either visualizing or modelling their temper to "fix" it.

To develop into an individual characterized by forbearance and understanding, one might consider emulating an individual who possesses the quality of composure rather than impulsivity. Do you have a particular admirer for their patience? Are there individuals to whom you can confide in times of stress?

You may choose a patient individual to serve as your model. Observe how they handle a situation that would ordinarily provoke you to anger. Can they effectively utilize both verbal and nonverbal cues? Can they exercise patience when dealing with difficult individuals? One potential approach is to inquire with a close acquaintance about their strategy for maintaining composure when confronted with pressures that would induce perspiration.

When an adequate number of observations have been accumulated, it becomes appropriate to commence modelling. You ought to devote some time to studying NLP. Close your eyes and consider an angry situation that could transpire. One possible source of anxiety is an irate clientele at the workplace or a recurring behaviour exhibited by one's children. Envision yourself to approach the given circumstance in your typical manner. This mental image might induce a small amount of internal frustration.

Consider the exact situation as if it were the model. Consider how they would approach the circumstance with composure and poise. Consider how they communicate, including their tone of voice and body language.

Recall that moment and envision yourself in that particular circumstance. This time, however, it is you who maintains your composure. Maintain awareness of your speech and the language you employ. As you visualize the situation, observe its progression. You will experience an increased sense of emotional and temper regulation. An internal reminder of your emotions and actions is possible to generate. Remaining composed of a few phrases, such as "stay calm," can assist you in regaining control of a novel circumstance.

If you are at a loss for an individual whose fortitude you admire, you may employ visualization to assist in temper management. Additionally, visualization can assist with anger management. This could be a hypothetical situation based on circumstances that provoke your rage or an actual occurrence that you cannot handle effectively.

After forming a mental image of the desired fury scenario, deconstruct it into more manageable components. Are you acquainted with the Choose Your Adventure novels in which each decision after a chapter or page affects the course of events in a unique way? The use of NLP visualization enables this. It empowers you to direct every aspect of your mental transformation. As you reflect on the scenario, your actions should come to mind. Make an effort to thoughtfully contemplate your words and conduct. Afterwards, contrast that behaviour with your typical conduct. Upon accomplishing a solution without resorting to wrath, direct your attention towards the emotion of pride.

You can envision yourself exhibiting the desired behaviour once you have achieved success. Applying the successes you have attained can prove beneficial in subsequent encounters with challenging circumstances that would ordinarily provoke you to lose your composure. One may recollect the refreshing sensation of maintaining composure while conversing in the same language employed during the visualization. It might require some effort and repetition to alter one's behaviour permanently. Nonetheless, cultivating mindfulness regarding one's thoughts and language can result in constructive transformations. While the preceding illustration pertained to a particular behaviour modification, identical methodologies can also be implemented to enhance other behaviours.

Consider how NPL can be implemented to enhance additional facets of one's self-concept. While responding to the inquiries at the commencement of this chapter, you may have become aware of an ailment within your own body. Numerous methods exist for enhancing one's physical appeal in the contemporary era. Cosmetics, surgery, and additional external procedures are included. However, these do not tackle the underlying factor contributing to your distress. NLP can facilitate a new perspective on oneself and guide one toward acceptance or a gratifying resolution.

NLP has the potential to assist individuals in altering their perception of a physical attribute that they associate with a diminished sense of self-worth. Neurolinguistic programming can assist by altering how your words and beliefs influence your behaviour. In this situation, the action to take is self-compassion. How can NLP assist you in altering your self-beliefs?

We shall begin with visualization. Reflect on the aspect of your appearance that you dislike the most. Direct your attention towards the unfavourable elements of your physical appearance through a mirror. Specify what it is. What is your stature? Your nostrils may be somewhat peculiar. The majority of individuals dislike some aspect of their nostrils. One's self-consciousness regarding appearance can influence outward presentation and interpersonal dynamics.

Concentrate on your tone of voice as you visualize your disapproval feature. For the sake of illustration, assume that the source of your discomfort is your nostril. Why? Consider the vocabulary you typically employ when describing your nostril to an unfamiliar individual. It is likely not particularly complimentary.

Consider possible replacements for your adjectives. Nonetheless, doing so has a positive connotation. Your nose is moderately sized. Consider more positive synonyms as an alternative. In NLP, language is crucial for enhancing one's self-concept. You must modify how you speak to and about yourself.

Embracing the imagery practised previously, position one's reflection in the mirror. You can now visualize yourself standing erect in your new language as your self-esteem increases and your self-awareness decreases. Observe the strength of your aquiline nostrils. It is regal, would you agree? This NLP exercise will instruct you to refresh your memory of the language each time you observe your reflection. You will quickly become accustomed to it and will no longer require self-reminders. Your conduct and sense of self will be irrevocably altered.

Additionally, NLP can resolve issues that impact one's appearance. Doing so would be possible; modelling could be applied here. There may be someone in your life whose appearance or physique matches yours. One could potentially emulate the beautification routines or exercise regimens that they observe.

Various personal transformations, including hairstyles, colours, apparel, tattoos, and makeup, can be envisioned through visualization. You can master NLP visualization to the point where you can depict virtually anything.

Define Dark Nlp.

Furthermore, your personality profile heavily influences the information that is processed and which information the mind chooses to exclude. Individuals who prioritize security perpetually evaluate their surroundings to ascertain whether they are secure enough to be there.

Conversely, individuals prioritizing freedom tend to perceive their circumstances solely regarding constraints and possibilities, not emphasize safety.

Your personality determines how you augment your mental library and, ultimately, the significance you ascribe to these internal maps. For instance, when a child observes a roller coaster, his or her sole concern is the enjoyment of riding in a stylish vehicle through a space. Should the opportunity present itself, the child would gladly and without hesitation board the ride, as his or her personality does not lean towards security.

However, a mature individual who can simultaneously appreciate the thrill and exhilaration of the ride and be mindful of its potential dangers and safety will reconsider that choice.

The following are notable NLP techniques:

Staple anchoring

Ivan Pavlov, a Russian scientist, experimented on canines. He determined he could induce salivation in dogs by repeatedly ringing a bell while they were eating, even without food.

The neurobiological association between the sound of the bell and the canines' salivation is called an "anchor" or "conditioned response."

Anchoring is establishing a discernible sensory stimulus corresponding to one's emotional state.

Consider giving it a try yourself! Visualize a bodily action or sensation—such as touching your forehead, raking your earlobe, or cracking your knuckles—and link it with a desired positive affective state—such as calmness, confidence, or joy—through the process of recollecting and reliving the memory in which you encountered those emotions in person.

The subsequent time you experience feelings of tension or depression, voluntarily activate this anchor, and you will observe an immediate shift in your mood. To strengthen the triggered response, one may recall and relive a memory in which they experienced the desired emotion.

As an additional memory is incorporated, the anchor will gain strength and elicit a more pronounced response.

Reframing Subjects

This NLP technique is most effectively utilized to counteract negative thoughts and emotions. By employing these visualization techniques, one can reprogram one's thoughts regarding circumstances that elicit feelings of vulnerability or helplessness.

Simply reframe the negative circumstance's significance into something positive. Consider the scenario where you recently severed ties with a long-term significant other or partner. You will likely sustain injuries and endure discomfort. However, it is possible to reframe the end of your relationship by focusing on the positive aspects of being single and the possibilities of new relationships.

You can concentrate on how the insights gained from your previous partnership can be applied to foster a more harmonious connection in the future. Simply reframing the breakup can help you feel better and regain your sense of agency.

This methodology has garnered significant attention in the realm of post-traumatic stress disorder treatment, as well as among individuals afflicted with chronic or life-threatening illnesses or those who have endured child abuse.

Rapport Development

Rapport-building is achieved through the use of cadence and mirroring the verbal and nonverbal behaviours of others to elicit empathy. Individuals have a preference for those they perceive to be similar to themselves.

When you can gradually mirror the other person, "pleasure sensors" or "mirror neurons" will activate in their brains, causing them to develop affection for you. You can simply adopt the other person's posture or seating position, turn your head in the same direction, or, even better, simply smile when they do. Each of these indicators will assist you in establishing rapport with the other individual. It is impossible to emphasize the social significance of rapport development enough. Robust personal and professional networks contribute to an extended and more contented existence.

A Separation

By employing the NLP dissociation technique, one can effectively disconnect negative emotions from the stimulus that elicits them. For example, specific words or expressions may elicit negative emotions and induce feelings of anxiety or depression. You will advance one stage toward self-healing and empowerment by effectively recognizing those stimuli and endeavouring to disentangle those detrimental emotions from them.

Using this method, a variety of mental health conditions, including anxiety, depression, and even phobias, can be effectively treated. It can also be applied positively to challenging circumstances at home and work.

Mind Regulation

An individual's mind serves as a sanctuary; upon incursion, the individual becomes completely susceptible to the assailant. There is a belief held by certain individuals that an external entity is incapable of claiming the psyche. They hold a firm conviction that the notion of mind control is purely imaginary.

Undoubtedly, many individuals hold the misconception that they possess complete control over their thoughts, even though this is patently false. It is possible that the initial instance of mind control in subliminal advertising took place in 1957. During a theatrical performance, a unique message was displayed on the screen. "You are thirsty," the message continued. Its rapid appearance and disappearance prevented anyone from noticing its presence. However, it had flickered approximately a thousand times by the time the film concluded. Nearly every audience member proceeded to the lobby after the film to purchase soft beverages. The initial experiment, meticulously monitored by scholars specializing in the enigma of the mind, employed the tachistoscope to convey the subliminal message to the audience members. Although the fleeting visual stimulus failed to register in the conscious mind, the subconscious diligently documented the incident. Over forty thousand moviegoers were exposed to the promotions "Drink Coca-Cola" and "Hungry? Eat Popcorn" during the initial six weeks of the experiment. The results of these experiments demonstrated that subliminal advertising is effective on the human psyche. Coca-Cola sales soared by nearly twenty per cent, while popcorn sales increased by sixty per cent. Despite not being hungry or thirsty, individuals were persuaded to purchase the advertised products through the subliminal advertising on the screen. However, moviegoers would assert they had complete mental control over the proceedings.

The human psyche is remarkably susceptible to manipulation and influence. The lighting, camera angle, and background music impact your thoughts and feelings while viewing a horror film. Despite being aware that the visual stimuli are not real, the brain continues reacting to the instructions presented. At times, one may experience a sense of dread in response to the graphic violence and gruesome scenes on the screen. Given the profound impact that conscious selection can have on the brain, one might wonder what kind of influence a seasoned dark psychological manipulator could exert.

Undetected mental control is the most difficult form of control that can be encountered. A person who recognizes that their mind is being controlled can reject the control in various ways, including physically, mentally, or verbally. To prevent themselves from falling prey to the controlling individual again, they will make every effort to avoid them. Individuals would typically flee in the face of a threat that they knew could infiltrate their minds and seize control of them. In the absence of detection or recognition of the mind controller, the victim will be defenceless against this psychological manipulation.

Two ways to gain mental control over another individual are through interpersonal communication or the media. Media mind control is typically feasible for sizable corporations. In contemporary times, however, the proliferation of laptops and smartphones has entrusted the most ruthless manipulators with the ability to control media.

Compared to other types of manipulators, undetected mind controllers typically appear more rational and timid. However, unlike impulsive psychopaths, detected mind controllers are more likely to act only after careful consideration. Undetectable mind control is not simple; it requires applying intentional knowledge and skill. Mind controllers are typically patient individuals because they gradually increase the extent of their dominion over the minds of others. Due to their frequent apprehension of being detected, they try to obscure their true intentions. They operate as shadowy puppet masters who persistently manipulate the strings of their victims without repercussions.

To exert covert control over the thoughts of their targets, proficient manipulators employ particular techniques. The media and interpersonal strategies comprise the manipulator's arsenal.

Acquiring a target with a specific objective is one of the most critical tactical methods of undetected mind control. Research has demonstrated that individuals who are in a state of distress are more susceptible to undetected mind control than those who are content and at peace with themselves and their community.

This can range from desires that appear to be unrelated, such as hunger or thirst, to largely pertinent objectives, such as carving love and affection.

When an individual is in quest of a companion among a group, they will eliminate those who do not contribute to their objectives and concentrate on the individual whose interests coincide with their own. The brain is comparable in this regard as well. It will direct an individual toward whatever he desires, even if that person is oblivious that a form of control is being exercised. The most proficient mind controllers will astutely discern their target's objectives before attempting to manipulate them with those goals in mind. When the human brain is programmed to experience a sense of desperation, it will promptly generate a recommendation regarding the particular item that should be selected.

Chapter 5: Methods for Recognizing External Manipulation

How To Recognize And Detect Manipulative Individuals

If you've ever felt that something is amiss in a casual relationship or that you're being coerced, controlled, or even made to feel like you're talking to yourself more than you should, it could be manipulation.

"Manipulation is a genuinely undesirable mental strategy utilized by people unequipped for requesting what they need in an immediate manner."Individuals who endeavour to dominate others strive to do so themselves.

A wide array of manipulation techniques exists, spanning from coercive salespeople to genuinely oppressive partners, and certain methods are more readily identifiable than others.

In this article, experts elucidate several symptoms that may indicate an individual is being manipulated: anxiety, commitment, and blame.

Three variables comprise manipulative behaviour: fear, commitment, and blame.

"When you are under the control of another individual, you are typically mentally coerced into performing an action that you would prefer not to. You might feel apprehensive about undertaking the task, obligated to complete it, or guilty of failing.

"The person in question" and "the domineering jerk" are the two frequent manipulators. A harasser potentially manipulates you through the use of hostility, threats, and terror to induce dread. The regrettable loss of life evokes a sense of guilt in the intended recipient. The injured person acts wounded the majority of the time. However, it is important to note that manipulators often assume the role of the victim when, in reality, they are the ones responsible for the situation.

An individual who is the target of manipulators and assumes the role of the aggrieved party will often endeavour to assist the manipulator in alleviating any remorse they may be feeling. Often, the manipulator feels obligated to assist the victim by doing anything in their power to alleviate their suffering.

Surprises are present.

The occurrence of anomalies may indicate the implementation of manipulation.

A manipulator of the first type is "Mr. Pleasant Guy." This person has the potential to be extremely helpful and perform an abundance of favours for others. It is perplexing because you are oblivious that something negative is occurring. However, conversely, every significant deed is accompanied by a string of desires. One who fails to satisfy the manipulator's whim will be characterized as self-centred.

Indeed, one of the most widely acknowledged forms of manipulation involves misusing correspondence standards and desires.

For example, a salesperson may manipulate the situation so that it appears as though the individual in question made an offer, compelling you to make a purchase; in a romantic partnership, an associate may influence you to the point where they require something from you that you are obligated to perform. These tactics are effective because they exploit societal norms. It is necessary to return favours.

Nevertheless, even when one is unscrupulously performed, we frequently feel obligated to provide our consent and response.

The 'foot-in-the-entranceway' and 'entranceway-in-the-face' techniques are apparent.

Manipulators frequently employ one of two strategies. One approach is the foot-in-the-entrance system, in which an individual initiates the conversation with a brief and practical inquiry, such as "Do you have the opportunity?" Which ultimately results in a more substantial request, such as "Ten dollars, please take me home for a taxi." This is frequently employed in road pranks. The entryway in-the-face strategy operates oppositely; it entails an individual submitting a substantial request, only to have it rejected, and then resubmit a minor one...

He explains that an individual engaged in contract work might approach you in advance with a substantial amount of money and then request a smaller amount after you decline. This is effective because the smaller request seems more practical in light of the larger solicitation.

Why Do Individuals Manipulate?

They exert control over you because they believe they will not be apprehended. Furthermore, they do not anticipate your intervention should they be apprehended.

What leads them to believe that they will not be captured? If you exhibit a lack of knowledge or susceptibility. They perceive themselves as possessing knowledge or comprehension that you do not.

Individuals who possess a limited understanding of social elements, struggle to comprehend jokes, fail to recognize a track until it is irretrievably damaged, are incapable of distinguishing greatness from lewd gestures, or are unable to distinguish between two people who are teasing will likely be subject to control by others simply because they can do so. They understand that it is impossible to care for something that you are unaware you are doing. They identify the deficiency and capitalize on it.

Furthermore, what rationale do they hold that you will remain motionless? Three factors contribute to this:

They may also exploit your ignorance to accuse you of instigating events or attempt to distract you with side arguments because they believe they can inflict more damage on you than you can on them; in reality, this is because you are probably overly amiable. They comprehend that a confrontation may render you unable to proceed further before separating because, through your carelessness, you have failed to establish commitments to counter deceit and any potential consequences. Unlike your manipulators, you convene a social gathering on behalf of your organization to engage in debates rather than seek support.

How am I to comprehend that? Becoming increasingly particularistic or less ethical are not viable solutions, in my opinion, as they fail to tackle the underlying causes of the problem. A viable and enduring strategy entails attending to all three areas of emphasis.

You must develop a deeper understanding of human instincts and inspirations. Commence by observing that many individuals are unmoved by ethical considerations, regardless of whether they anticipate receiving compensation for doing the right thing or being reprimanded for an unethical act. This means that if you demonstrate deficiencies and offer a minimal probability of retaliation, it is inconsequential where you are or with whom you are; someone will handle that.

Acquire the skill of ardent equalization and detachment of desires so that you are truly impervious to harm from most things. It is unwise to expect the best from others; doing so exposes oneself to the possibility of manipulation.

Develop an increasing awareness of social components. Recognize that certain individuals form close friendships for social validation rather than out of admiration or loyalty to the organization.

A considerable number of individuals whom I am currently acquainted with have, for obvious reasons, been subjected to the severe tactics of manipulation – which includes practices that defy human explanation and clarification, obsessive lies that are over the top, and the dreadful results of triangulations and slanderous attacks – as well as love-besieging.

These entities operate under the pretext of' manipulation.'

Consequently, why do a select few individuals employ manipulation as a tactic?

What exactly motivates individuals to exert control rather than act in good faith?

I would like to accompany you on an excursion to gain a more comprehensive understanding of manipulation.'

Utilizing NLP In Mentoring

The utilisation of NLP is on the rise among life and sports coaches. The objective is to concentrate on the subject's accomplishments in particular skills or objectives. Again, the issue that will be resolved is filters in general. Skills and objectives are associated with mental states and internal representations. Filters regulate how they manifest. Consequently, modify the filter, state, and representation.

A number of the methodologies employed in mental health contexts are also applicable in this context. Aside from working with mental disorders that fall under the purview of mental health laws, however, the utilisation of NLP for coaching presents an abundance of opportunities for the ambitious NLP practitioner. Colleagues of mine have utilised their expertise in natural language processing (NLP) to assist academically struggling children and highly compensated professional athletes.

As described, the disintegrating anchor technique is an excellent one to employ when limiting beliefs appear to be the issue. Assisting a quarterback in enhancing his passing ability is a plausible application of this concept. Additionally, I appreciate the diverse timeline techniques employed by practitioners. As an illustration, a physical timeline could be constructed in a hallway, the subject directed to revisit a moment of optimal performance, and an anchor word or keyword could be generated.

Then, instruct them to advance in time to the subsequent occasion they must execute the identical mission. Release the anchor once they have reached that position and observe the physiological change again. This extremely straightforward method may be implemented in a coaching context.

Indicators of Unstable

Six indications, as identified by experts, that your instabilities are impacting your relationships are provided below.

Our concern with "not having sufficient" or "not being enough" generates instability. The source of these anxieties is vanity. When we lack confidence, we are preoccupied with the opinions of others and lack a robust sense of self and healthy self-esteem. Below are a few signs of instability that may suggest you need to silence your ego and be authentically yourself.

1. Displaying

One of the most prevalent signs of instability is taking pride in one's possessions and accomplishments.

Troubled individuals have a propensity to attempt to excite others. They ultimately become destitute in terms of garnering recognition from the external world. However, those with a secure sense of self do not consistently perceive the need to provoke others. Furthermore, others don't have to validate you.

2. Controlling

At times, individuals who are being monitored may exhibit signs of stability. However, the source of controlling behaviour is both anxiety and insecurity. This is among the most prevalent signs that suggest instability. We scramble to control and maintain appropriate boundaries worldwide to feel risk-free, safe, and secure. This may cause us to exert control over others, as we will only feel secure when they behave in predictable ways. When we realise that we can handle any circumstance that may arise in life, we no longer feel the need to rigorously regulate every aspect to feel secure. We can then embrace life's muddled splendour and move with the flow.

3. Anxiety and Stress

Anxiety is frequently precipitated by a feeling of inadequacy as well. When we are apprehensive, we frequently fear what others might think of us or are so terrified that we are certain to cause some sort of destruction. Individuals who are secure in their own persona experience reduced levels of anxiety regarding points. This is because they do not consistently prioritise accuracy. While they may continue to hold themselves to high standards, they do not condemn themselves for each perceived error. They accept that, being human, they will frequently make mistakes and that this is acceptable.

4. Compelling Individuals

A conspicuous indication of instability is an unwavering preoccupation with pleasing others. This prevents you from living your existence. Consistently striving to bring happiness to others may, at times, give the impression that your existence is not your own. Individuals with a high sense of self-esteem demonstrate compassion and care for others but do not hold themselves responsible for the welfare of others. Indeed, that is true. You have no bearing on the happiness of others and are not obligated to protect or rescue them from every negative experience they may have.

Individuals who are people-pleasers must allocate time and attention to their own needs and desires. You must obtain the possibility to do the things that make you joyful and follow your desires and not merely assist others in accomplishing theirs. On the other hand, people-pleasing may lead to resentment and even a sense of martyrdom. This is not a balanced and healthful way to be.

People-pleasing is detrimental to one's development and the development of others, which is frequently unfavourable for them.

5. Occasionalism

Possessing an attitude in which nothing you do is satisfactory or devoting excessive time to achieving "perfect" points could indicate insecurity. This generally manifests as an apprehension towards criticism or failure. You find it difficult to relinquish and move on from a task out of concern that the final result may not meet your expectations. Unfortunately, this could lead to getting trapped, never completing tasks, or devoting excessive time to any endeavour. This can suggest you cease working to meet due dates or disappoint people. This is detrimental to one's self-esteem and may lead to a downward trajectory. Though perfectionism can be difficult to overcome, the starting point is to maintain a positive and balanced self-perception and to be compassionate and more accepting of oneself.

Anxiety 6.

Anxiety frequently serves as an indicator of insecurity. Clinical depression may manifest as an individual withdraws from life due to an accumulation of tension. Often, stress compels us to withdraw from the world to avoid harm, criticism, or failure. By cultivating a robust sense of self-awareness, one can independently confront the world without experiencing excessive anxiety and distress. Undoubtedly, recovering from stress is not always a simple task; nevertheless, commencing with minor self-care practices and practising self-compassion is an exceptional strategy to initiate the process of overcoming debilitating clinical depression.

Varieties Of NLP Education

If you are looking for NLP training, you might be contemplating which type suits your needs. The selection of NLP training will also impact the amount of time dedicated to self-study regarding the training. For specific individuals, the duration can span from days to years.

In general, two varieties of NLP preparation are available. This includes both drenching learning and homeroom-style instruction. Both techniques conclude with affirmation, along with their respective advantages and disadvantages.

Study hall-style learning allows for the dispersion of NLP courses over weeks or months. A course may be attended twice weekly for six months, enabling many individuals to budget for educational expenses while progressing quickly. Despite this, there are disadvantages associated with this method of learning. Because the classes are so protracted and time-consuming, certain individuals will likely be unable to complete them due to life circumstances, such as constantly relocating to find employment or having a child. Even if it has been several days since the last class, a significant portion of one class can be devoted to recapitulation and reinforcing material covered in the previous class. Additionally, the necessity to neglect core courses may result in knowledge gaps regarding NLP.

A process known as "quickened learning" or "submersion learning" can be significantly more efficient. This type of NLP preparation requires you to set aside 21 days out of your life, spanning multiple weeks, to completely immerse yourself in learning everything there is to know about NLP. Positive aspects of this learning approach include the elimination of gaps in one's understanding, which can be attributed to the intensive and exhaustive nature of the courses. A few individuals struggling to learn must be given additional opportunities to scrutinize and "sink in" the information.

Although it is possible to educate oneself through traditional NLP preparation and courses, additional seminars, courses, books, and accounts are constantly published that provide the opportunity to enhance one's NLP preparation skills. NLP is a skill that requires daily cultivation; inadvertently, many individuals who undertake NLP training discover that opportunities to better themselves present themselves daily. This is because the fundamental concept of NLP is to become increasingly receptive to experiences that are advantageous to oneself. This ongoing learning process spans an entire life, and consistent practice of natural language processing (NLP) will ultimately result in a more prosperous existence with additional lucrative connections.

Who Develops NLP Skills?

A wide array of professions can derive legitimate benefits from implementing NLP preparation. Many individuals pursue coaching primarily to influence their progress and become more captivating and influential. The desire to become an increasingly successful, well-organized, and genuinely secure person is an admirable goal in and of itself.

Additionally, one can obtain accreditation to teach NLP training to others; this is a significant benefit if an educational institution or a business employs one. When managers encounter this on your resume, they will discern that you have made an effort to enhance your interpersonal skills and that you are possibly a competent leader who understands how to motivate others and accomplish objectives.

The field of instruction stands to gain significantly from NLP preparation. Physical mentors and holistic mentors benefit tremendously from NLP, primarily because a substantial portion of their daily work consists of motivating others to surpass their own performance expectations.

Additionally, therapists and advisers of all types can employ the skills they acquire through NLP training to motivate and inspire individuals who are depressed, hopeless, or afflicted. NLP can also be utilized by depression advocates, addiction counsellors, and specialists attempting to motivate a person to create a more positive existence following a personal catastrophe.

Educators may also employ the strategies and competencies employed in NLP training to motivate struggling students or to develop into more persuasive public speakers. Business leaders can employ these skills to engage in more meaningful conversations with their employees and, if involved in negotiations, enhance their offerings and profits by precisely comprehending the factors influencing consumers to purchase their products.

If you are interested in career progression or establishing yourself as a prospective representative, then enrolling in NLP training can effectively impress the leader. Every aspect of your persona will appear increasingly practical and proficient. You will surpass expectations upon meeting the board and develop into the definitive figurehead of a mature, competent, and dependable individual. Your vitality is liberated to concentrate on propelling yourself forward in daily life, as your mind is no longer clouded with the "dramatization of the day" or preoccupied with domestic concerns.

Ultimately, individuals who engage in NLP training significantly improve in emergencies compared to those who do not. They possess experience in adopting a strategic perspective and properly executing well-executed developments. An individual who has received NLP training is less likely to experience failure, lead a group astray, or be unemployed for an extended period due to the development of their adaptability in the face of new circumstances. The NLP veteran is perpetually on the brink of crisis readiness and cannot merely recover from a setback; they can also salvage a disastrous situation to benefit all parties involved.

Chapter 4: Success is attained through modelling

In addition to being a technique with limitless potential for combination with other patterns, modelling is a method that never becomes repetitive. We will develop a greater desire to accomplish as we attain mastery in our respective disciplines; this is related to emulating subsequent attitudes, habits, ways of thinking, action plans, and, ultimately, specific tasks that bring us closer and closer to our ideal destination. Success is achieved through modelling because it enables us to realize our maximum potential and creates a legacy of not one but numerous accomplishments throughout our lives. It is advisable to strive for success at this moment, gaining knowledge from the most accomplished individuals in your industry to attain their level of expertise. It is a method that motivates you to improve yourself and positively influence others.

Frequently, those who attain great success are virtuous individuals who adhere to fair play and honestly regard their adversaries. We can adopt positive attitudes that will benefit both ourselves and our environment, which may be motivated by the positive attitudes exhibited through modelling. Ultimately, modelling is a virtuous cycle in which individuals motivate one another, uplifting entire communities and rendering them more virtuous, educated, or simply more effective.

It is worthwhile to attempt this method. Positive outcomes can result from assuming control of positive patterns, just as negative patterns, such as succumbing to stimulants, sloth, or disorganization, can be conquered with constructive intentions. We can become more efficient and effective by learning to organize our lives better. This is incomparably preferable to forming negative patterns, which impede our progress and lead us to our demise rather than our ascent. Attempting everything that emerges and, notwithstanding setbacks, regarding them as learning opportunities is commendable.

While less desirable than achievements, this is an essential aspect of growth. Even the most accomplished individuals in history have pursued mastery through trial and error, determining which approaches are effective and which fail. One does not have to repeat past errors by having readily available strategies for achieving success; rather, one can cultivate expertise and expand one's knowledge across various domains.

Consider a few individuals who employ dark psychology techniques the most.

1. Salespeople—These individuals are the most frequent consumers we encounter daily. They employ various persuasive techniques, including advertisements, door-to-door campaigns, and professional language, to influence consumers to buy their products. This pertains primarily to salesmen who are so intent on achieving a specific goal that they will do anything to convince customers to purchase their products.

2. Individuals classified as sociopaths based on clinical diagnosis – True

psychopathic individuals are devoid of both remorse and an emotional sensibility. Conversely, these individuals are frequently generous, intelligent, and impulsive. They capitalize on these qualities by employing dark psychology strategies to cultivate exceptionally robust connections with individuals they exploit without remorse.

3. Lawyers – Most solicitors are intent on prevailing in court. Therefore, they employ any strategy possible to achieve the desired results. Certain legal professionals employ nefarious persuasion methods.

Narcissists, number four Individuals who satisfy the clinical criteria for the label narcissist possess an exaggerated perception of their value. Typically, they require external validation and ego-stroking. Narcissists desire for others to perceive them as inferior to themselves. His or her fundamental wish is to be excessively adored and worshipped. To gain adherents, the narcissist will employ any strategy possible, including manipulation based on dark psychology and unethical practices.

Many politicians are self-centred and will do anything to secure votes. They occasionally employ dark psychology techniques to persuade others of their position.

6. Leaders—A subset of leaders and administrators employs deceitful strategies to coerce others into doing as they desire.

7. Selfish individuals – Certain individuals are motivated solely by self-interest and will do anything to achieve their objectives. These individuals may occasionally employ tactics to satisfy their desires without regard for the repercussions on others.

8. Public speakers – One might inquire how an individual with the benevolent intention of assisting others in their personal growth could employ nefarious strategies. Indeed, they may. Certain presenters may employ dubious strategies to increase their following or sell more products.

While acknowledging the potential for offending by mentioning the individuals above, it is critical to have a foundational understanding. All individuals, including attorneys, public speakers, salespeople, and leaders, strive to earn a livelihood. Nonetheless, they must be truthful regarding their work and refrain from employing manipulative strategies. As a potential victim, you must possess the ability to discern whether an individual is employing dark psychology and manipulative tactics with good or evil intentions.

A salesperson can essentially increase a company's revenue through dark psychology and manipulative strategies. Certain sales representatives even acknowledge that their employers instruct and mandate the use of dark psychology to achieve goals and acquire and retain clients. This is highly regrettable, as while the organization may generate revenue, it will ultimately result in substandard business practices, scepticism, low employee loyalty, and diminished long-term viability.

To discern between motivations and persuasion techniques that are ethical and unethical, it is critical to evaluate one's intentions. You must consider whether these techniques benefit all of us or whether they are beneficial for only one individual. It is acceptable for these techniques to benefit you in conjunction with others; however, their use for one's benefit is considered unethical. One can easily succumb to sinister techniques when motivated solely by self-interest.

Conscious use of dark psychology must be avoided by striving for a win-win circumstance. The primary objective of a salesperson ought to be to sell a product that provides value to the consumer. He or she must have the capacity to be truthful with the consumer. The primary objective of the salesperson is to inform the prospective consumer about the advantages of the products to persuade him or her to make a purchase.

It is crucial that individuals in leadership, sales, marketing, or any other relevant role refrain from employing dark psychology techniques for self-serving objectives.

What is my objective or intention regarding this interaction?

Do my actions contribute to the betterment of others, or am I the only beneficiary?

Do I have a positive perception of my approach to this interaction?

Am I completely candid and forthright with the other individual?

Will the outcomes of this dialogue prove advantageous for all parties involved in the long run?

Will I develop a more sustainable and reliable relationship with this individual?

Such introspection will assist an individual in refraining from employing self-centred, dark psychology methods on others. You must evaluate your existing strategies for inspiration and persuasion to achieve genuine success in various domains such as parenting, leadership, relationships, and the workplace. Ethical conduct will result in a sustained favourable reception and enhanced credibility. You may temporarily achieve your goals by employing sinister techniques, but doing so will cost you in the long run: shattered relationships, diminished credibility, and poor character because others can see through your deceit.

Consider the growing interest in dark psychology and the methods for identifying its practitioners. Increasing numbers of individuals are acquiring emotional intelligence to evade manipulation and unethical manipulation.

In What Way Does Hypnosis Benefit You?

The utilization of stage hypnosis could potentially tarnish the process unjustly. As previously stated, an adequately trained stage hypnotist possesses not only the ability to deliver an outstanding performance but also the knowledge necessary to handle any circumstance that may arise. Nevertheless, if one requires hypnotherapy, forsaking a private consultation in favour of voluntarily participating in a periodic hypnosis demonstration is preferable. The integration of hypnotherapy into evidence-based therapy is on the rise, and it has emerged as a clinical practice standard. It finds application in the management of pain, promotion of weight reduction, therapy for sleep disorders, anxiety, depression, and sports psychology. It is especially effective when combined with cognitive-behavioural therapy, as it equips the clinician with techniques to address conscious and unconscious thoughts and beliefs.

Surprising Hypnosis Facts You Never Knew

Throughout the film, audience members witnessed hypnotists wielding gold pocket watches and murmuring, "You are all tired. Overly drowsy." However, were you aware that hypnosis can be employed as a therapeutic technique? Patients may utilize hypnotics administered by a well-trained hypnotherapist to overcome addiction, recover from traumatic experiences, and enhance their overall quality of life. Even though the facts may appear a little unsettling or magical, the operation of hypnosis is quite scientific. Edie Raether, a hypnotherapist and behavioural psychologist with an MS, CSP, stated to Bustle, "Alpha brainwave activity induces individuals to enter a state of relaxation." "As a result of relaxation, clients are more receptive and open in this contemplative state."

Once the client is at ease, the hypnotherapist can assist them in attaining the desired improvement in their condition. "There are two distinct types of hypnosis: exploratory and suggestive," stated Raether. It exhibits remarkable efficacy in the treatment of PTSD (post-traumatic stress disorder). "Subconscious and latent experiences surfaced and expelled, allowing people to recover immediately."

It is effective because the underlying issue is initially recognized and resolved. According to Raether: "In the right hands, composed of a well-known and experienced therapist, this is indeed the most economical and effective way to change any behaviour (including academic and sports performance)." An expert stated that additional intriguing occurrences could transpire throughout the hypnotherapy.

A shift will occur in your consciousness.

Individuals under hypnosis may appear to be "asleep" or "not in" when, in fact, they are partitioning their consciousness or fantasizing. Hypnotherapist Darlene Corbett stated to Bustle, "Hypnosis is a process of separation; there has been a modification in the state of consciousness." "What happens in the brain is like in a daydream."

After an individual achieves a state of deep relaxation and dreaminess, the hypnotherapist can initiate the process of resolving their latent issues. "The subject of all attention is hypnosis," Corbett stated. "Because of their ability to focus, they can use many areas of authorization that they are not aware of."

You have hygienized yourself technically.

While it may appear that the hypnotherapist is performing all the work or "making" the subject hypnotized, it is the subject who is relaxing.

Anthony Gitch of RHT of Excel Hypnosis told Bustle, "Every instance of hypnosis is self-hypnosis." "Moreover, you do not have to engage in this action. "This involves a delicate interplay between the therapist and the subconscious mind, in which the therapist guides the subconscious mind to generate profound internal insights." Pretty cool, right?

You Might Feel Light or Heavy.

In hypnosis, there is no "correct" method to experience emotion. Gucci indicated, "Either hypnotizes nothing, or feels heavy, or feels very light." "It's unimportant because this is your experience, and you will experience exactly what you need."

The "Mind-Controlled" Will Not Appear.

People who are interested in attempting hypnosis may find solace in the fact that while it may be an unusual sensation, it is not mind control. According to Gitch: "The hypnotist cannot make someone do something against their will." Being who you are enables you to maintain absolute control over your department.

The Change Might Be Felt in a Single Class.

Contrary to popular belief, it is not possible to induce or maintain a minor hypnotic state after the conclusion of the meeting. However, you might only wish to experience it once, Gucci advised, given that numerous individuals find it calming and comforting.

When you depart, however, you may encounter substantial changes. Rather stated, "I have witnessed 85 per cent of smokers quit following a course of treatment." However, this measure of success is only possible for those who permit it.

Reiser commented: "If people just stay there and need to stick to their defences to cope and function, then it is wise to try hypnotherapy." "In the presence of emotionally vulnerable individuals, exploratory hypnosis is not something I engage in." Additionally, carry additional items that may surpass their capability." Rather, she stated that she would assist clients in developing self-assurance and resiliency before attempting hypnosis. Consequently, they will have enhanced capabilities to manage all that they have unblocked.

www.ingramcontent.com/pod-product-compliance
Lightning Source LLC
Chambersburg PA
CBHW052133110526
44591CB00012B/1700